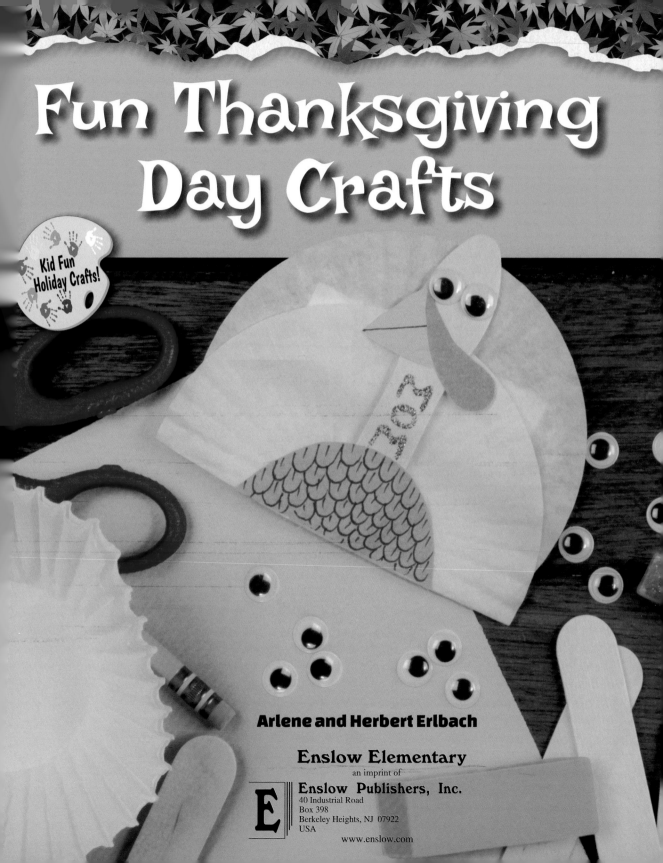

Fun Thanksgiving Day Crafts

Kid Fun Holiday Crafts!

Arlene and Herbert Erlbach

Enslow Elementary

an imprint of

Enslow Publishers, Inc.

40 Industrial Road
Box 398
Berkeley Heights, NJ 07922
USA

www.enslow.com

Enslow Elementary, an imprint of Enslow Publishers, Inc.
Enslow Elementary® is a registered trademark of Enslow Publishers, Inc.

Originally published as *Thanksgiving Day Crafts* in 2005.

Library of Congress Cataloging-in-Publication Data
Erlbach, Arlene.
  [Thanksgiving Day crafts]
  Fun Thanksgiving Day crafts / Arlene and Herbert Erlbach.
     pages cm. — (Kid fun holiday crafts!)
  Includes bibliographical references and index.
  Audience: Grades K to grade 3.
  ISBN 978-0-7660-6250-4
  1. Thanksgiving decorations—Juvenile literature. I. Erlbach, Herb. II. Title.
  TT900.T5E75 2015
  745.594'1649—dc23
                        2014024704

Summary: "Explains the origins of Thanksgiving and how to make ten holiday-related crafts"—Provided by publisher.

Future editions:
Paperback ISBN: 978-0-7660-6251-1
EPUB ISBN: 978-0-7660-6252-8
Single-User PDF ISBN: 978-0-7660-6253-5
Multi-User PDF ISBN: 978-0-7660-6254-2

Printed in the United States of America

102014 Bang Printing, Brainerd, Minn.

10 9 8 7 6 5 4 3 2 1

To Our Readers: We have done our best to make sure all Internet addresses in this book were active and appropriate when we went to press. However, the author and the publisher have no control over and assume no liability for the material available on those Internet sites or on other Web sites they may link to. Any comments or suggestions can be sent by e-mail to comments@enslow.com or to the address on the back cover.

♻ Enslow Publishers, Inc., is committed to printing our books on recycled paper. The paper in every book contains 10% to 30% post-consumer waste (PCW). The cover board on the outside of each book contains 100% PCW. Our goal is to do our part to help young people and the environment too!

Illustration Credits: Crafts prepared by June Ponte; craft photography by Carl Feryok; Corel Corporation, p. 5.

Cover Illustration: Craft prepared by June Ponte; craft photography by Kristin McCarthy and Carl Feryok.

CONTENTS

Safety Note: Be sure to ask for help from an adult, if needed, to complete these crafts!

INTRODUCTION

The fourth Thursday in November is a special date to people in the United States of America. It is Thanksgiving. It is the day when people get together with their family and friends to give thanks. It is also a time to remember the Pilgrims' first harvest in 1621.

Thanksgiving did not become an annual American holiday for many years after the Pilgrims' first Thanksgiving. During colonial times, days of thanksgiving were celebrated when there were good harvests and other happy events. George Washington declared a day of Thanksgiving be observed on November 26, 1789. In the years that followed, many states had Thanksgiving celebrations.

The tradition of observing Thanksgiving as a national holiday on the fourth Thursday in November did not happen until 1863. A magazine editor named Sarah Josepha Hale is

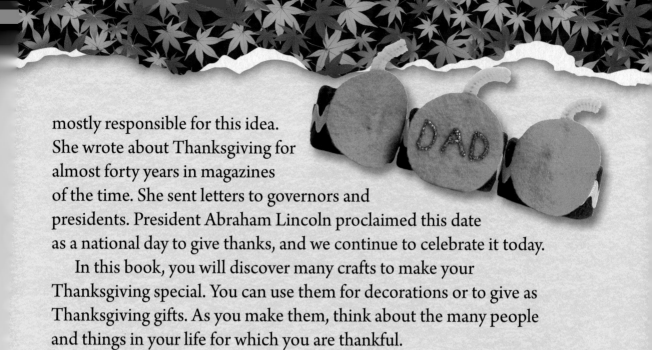

mostly responsible for this idea. She wrote about Thanksgiving for almost forty years in magazines of the time. She sent letters to governors and presidents. President Abraham Lincoln proclaimed this date as a national day to give thanks, and we continue to celebrate it today.

In this book, you will discover many crafts to make your Thanksgiving special. You can use them for decorations or to give as Thanksgiving gifts. As you make them, think about the many people and things in your life for which you are thankful.

Miniature Pilgrims

These Pilgrims have empty film canisters for their bodies. Make a Pilgrim boy and girl to decorate your Thanksgiving table.

What You Will Need (for two pilgrims)

- scissors
- cotton swab
- red crayon or marker
- glue
- wiggle eyes
- film canisters
- sheets of black, white, pink, and brown construction paper
- glitter
- yarn

What to do

1. Cut black construction paper into two strips, each 2 by 4 inches. Glue one of the 2-by-4-inch strips to each film canister. Trim, if necessary.

2. Cut two more strips from the black paper. These strips should measure 1 by 3 inches. Glue the middle of each strip to the back of each canister to form the Pilgrim's arms.

3. Cut construction paper to form heads and small round circles for hands. Glue on wiggle eyes and draw a smile on each. Attach the heads and hands to the canisters with glue.

4. Cut white paper to form the boy's collar. (You can use the pattern on page 27.) Glue it to the boy's coat.

5. Trace the pattern on page 27 for the boy's hat. Cut a piece of black construction paper 1¾ inch long by ½ inch high for the brim. Glue them together. Draw a glitter "buckle" on the front of the hat.

6. Cut two pieces of white paper to form the girl's cap and apron. Attach the apron and cap with glue. Add yarn or cut paper fringe for the hair. Let dry.

Wrap the black paper around
the film canisters . . .

Add the arms . . .

The hands and faces
are next . . .

Your pilgrims are ready for the table!

HOLIDAY HINT:

If you wish, make enough Pilgrim
figures to use as individual party
favors. Display your Pilgrims to
remind you of Thanksgiving.

Rocking Miniature Mayflower

This *Mayflower* rocks when you tap an end with your finger. You can use it as a centerpiece with the miniature Pilgrims.

What You Will Need

- ❀ scissors
- ❀ paper plate
- ❀ pencil
- ❀ brown and white construction paper
- ❀ glue
- ❀ craft sticks
- ❀ crayons or markers

What to Do

1. Place a folded plate on the brown paper. Draw two half circles on the paper around the paper plate.

2. Cut out both half-circles. Do not cut the plate. Use a crayon or marker to draw lines that will look like wood on the construction paper. Set the half-circles aside.

3. Use the sail patterns on page 27 to draw sails on the white paper. Cut them out.

4. On the main sail, print "Happy Thanksgiving" or other Thanksgiving messages.

5. Cut a small strip of white paper to form the ship's flag.

6. Glue one stick to the center and one stick to each end of the paper plate halves. This way your ship will balance.

7. Glue one of the brown paper half-circles over the side of the plate with the craft sticks glued to it. Glue the second half-circle to the other side of the plate.

8. Attach the sails to the craft sticks with glue.

9. When your *Mayflower* is dry, tap the edges. It will rock like a ship on the stormy sea.

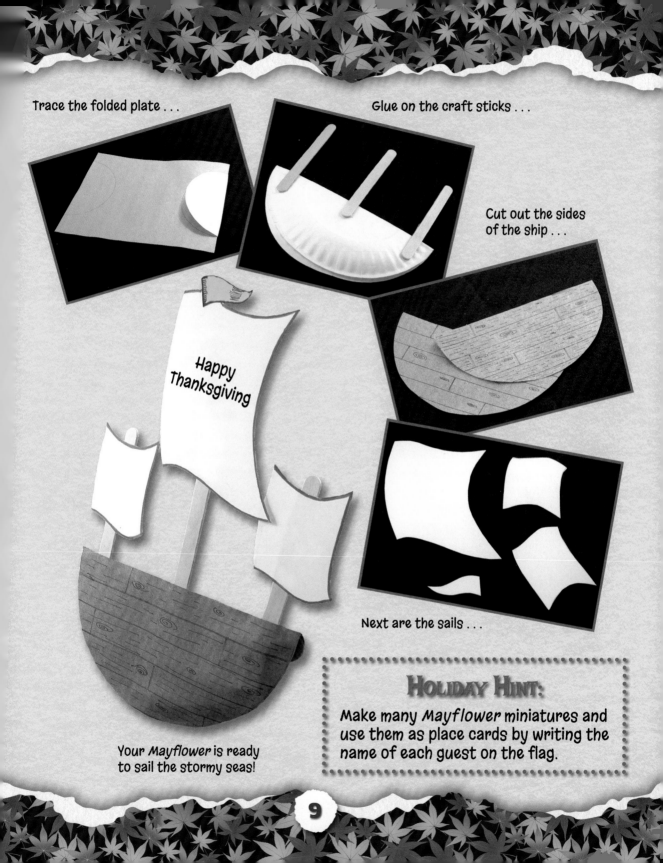

Trace the folded plate . . .

Glue on the craft sticks . . .

Cut out the sides
of the ship . . .

Happy
Thanksgiving

Next are the sails . . .

Your *Mayflower* is ready
to sail the stormy seas!

HOLIDAY HINT:

Make many *Mayflower* miniatures and
use them as place cards by writing the
name of each guest on the flag.

Beaded Corn Pin or Magnet

Corn is one of the crops that American Indians taught the Pilgrims how to plant. Make a corn pin or corn magnet to celebrate this important crop.

What You Will Need

- ❋ scissors
- ❋ yellow, orange, and green pony beads or tri-beads
- ❋ cotton swab
- ❋ pipe cleaners cut into 6-inch pieces
- ❋ brown construction paper
- ❋ craft glue
- ❋ ribbon or yarn in a contrasting color
- ❋ a pin backing or magnetic tape

What to Do

1. String eight beads onto each piece of pipe cleaner to form corncobs. Leave about a ¼-inch of pipe cleaner on the bottom of each cob. Leave about 1 inch on the top.

2. Fold a ¼-inch portion of pipe cleaner over the corncobs. Dab on glue to attach the folded portion of the pipe cleaner to the corn. This will hold the beads together on the bottom.

3. Twist the pipe cleaners on top as shown to hold the cobs of corn together on the top.

4. Cut construction paper into 4-by-4-inch pieces and fold it to create the husk. Glue it to the top of the corncobs.

5. Add ribbon or yarn.

6. Attach magnetic tape to the back of the corn to make a magnet. Glue on a pin backing to make a pin to wear.

Slide beads onto the
pipe cleaners . . .

Twist the pipe
cleaners together . . .

Display the beaded corn for all
your family and friends to see!

HOLIDAY HINT:

Wear your corn pin or
use it as a refrigerator
magnet.

Fall Tree Collage

A collage is a design made by pasting paper, cloth, and other things in an arrangement on a surface. This tree collage features brightly colored leaves made from tissue paper.

What you will need

- scissors
- glue
- a paper edger (optional)
- pencil
- black, brown, and orange construction paper
- tissue paper in fall colors

What to do

1. Draw a tree on the brown paper. (You can use the pattern on page 28.) Cut out the tree.

2. Glue the tree to the black paper. Tear and cut tissue paper to form the leaves.

3. Glue your leaves onto the tree branches. Glue some of the leaves so they look like they are falling, or have fallen, to the ground. Let dry.

4. When your collage is complete, cut around the edge of your paper. A paper edger, if you have one, creates an attractive effect. Glue the collage to a sheet of orange paper.

Draw a tree . . .

Carefully cut it out . . .

Glue it on another paper
and add the leaves . . .

Your collage is ready
for display!

HOLIDAY HINT:
You can hang your tree collage
on your front door as a welcome
sign for Thanksgiving.

Leaves in the Wind Glitter Globe

In many parts of the country, trees have lost their leaves by November. Make your own leaf globe.

What you will need

* newspaper to protect your workspace
* scissors
* large, clean, and dry baby food jars with lids. Remove the labels.
* cotton swabs
* fabric in a fall color
* pencil
* silicon-based (waterproof) glue
* water
* glitter
* foil confetti in leaf shapes
* baby oil (optional)

What to do

1. Place the jar's lid on the fabric. Draw around the lid of the jar with the pencil. Cut it out and set aside. This will be the lid's covering.

2. Fill your jar with water. Add the baby oil if you plan to use it. The oil will make the leaves flow more slowly in the jar.

3. Add about ten confetti leaves to the jar.

4. Add a pinch of glitter. Be careful not to add too much glitter, or you will not be able to see the leaves flow through the jar.

5. Dab the glue around the inside of the lid with the cotton swab. Screw the lid on securely. Make sure that the jar is shut tightly. Dry overnight.

6. Glue the cut fabric to the top of the lid. Let dry.

7. Dab glue around the edge of the lid with a cotton swab. You may want to glue some glitter and pieces of confetti on the top. Let dry.

8. Shake your glitter globe and watch the leaves flutter and float.

First, make the
lid cover . . .

Add the confetti leaves
and glitter . . .

Glue the lid closed and glue
on the fabric cover . . .

Give it a good shake and watch the
glitter and leaves float around!

HOLIDAY HINT:

Make a glitter globe as
a present for someone
that you are grateful
to have in your life.

LEAF PLAQUE

You will use the dry brush technique of painting to create the leaf on your plaque.

WHAT YOU WILL NEED

- ❀ newspaper
- ❀ paper plate
- ❀ paintbrush
- ❀ brown construction paper
- ❀ pencil
- ❀ tissue paper
- ❀ hole punch
- ❀ glue
- ❀ scissors
- ❀ poster paint in fall colors like orange and yellow
- ❀ plastic bowls
- ❀ a leaf (optional)
- ❀ yarn or ribbon
- ❀ white paper
- ❀ scrap paper

WHAT TO DO

1. Cover your worktable with newspaper.

2. Cover the paper plate with tissue paper. This will be the background for your painted leaf. Punch a hole at the top and set it aside.

3. Trace a leaf on the brown paper or use the pattern on page 26. Cut it out.

4. Pour paint into bowls. Dip your paintbrush into one color. Make brush strokes on the scrap paper until the paintbrush is almost dry. Brush the color onto the edges of your leaf. Wash your brush. Dip your paint into another color and repeat. You can brush colors over colors, if you like.

5. When you are satisfied with your dry brush leaf, let it dry completely. Then glue it to the paper plate background.

6. Loop the yarn through the hole. Your leaf plaque is ready to display.

Cover the paper plate with tissue paper . . .

Trace the leaf and cut it out . . .

Paint the leaf fall colors . . .

Add some yarn at the top and your plaque is ready to be hung up!

Scarecrow

Farmers place scarecrows in cornfields to frighten hungry birds away from their crops. This scarecrow will not scare anybody. You can wear it, use it as a magnet, or use it as a decoration.

What you will need

- ❀ scissors
- ❀ fine-tipped marker
- ❀ cotton swab
- ❀ scraps of fabric or construction paper
- ❀ craft glue
- ❀ craft spoon
- ❀ craft sticks
- ❀ straw, or brown or yellow shredded paper
- ❀ wiggle eyes
- ❀ magnetic tape or a pin backing

What to do

1. Glue the craft stick to the center of the craft spoon as shown. This will form the scarecrow's body.

2. Trace a hat, shirt, and pants onto fabric or construction paper. You can use the patterns on page 26. Cut them out. Glue the shirt and pants to the scarecrow's body.

3. Glue on the wiggle eyes, and draw the scarecrow's mouth with the marker. Add the hat.

4. Glue the straw or shredded paper to the scarecrow's clothing.

5. Add the pin backing to make a pin to wear. Add magnetic tape to make a magnet.

Glue the sticks together and then glue on the shirt and pants . . .

Next comes the hat and face . . .

Your scarecrow is ready to wear!

HOLIDAY HINT:

Add the scarecrow to your other Thanksgiving decorations.

Pumpkin Napkin Rings

Pumpkins are a popular Thanksgiving decoration. Pumpkin was eaten by the Pilgrims at the first Thanksgiving. Make some pumpkin napkin rings to celebrate the season.

What you will need

- scissors
- a toilet paper tube
- green and orange felt
- pipe cleaners
- tacky glue
- rickrack (optional)

What to do

1. Squeeze the toilet paper tube flat and cut it into 1-inch sections.

2. Cut the orange felt into circles. These will be your pumpkins.

3. Cut the pipe cleaners into 2-inch pieces. Glue a piece of pipe cleaner onto the back of each pumpkin so that the stem sticks up over the pumpkin.

4. Cut the green felt into 1½- by 6-inch strips. Glue each strip to a piece of toilet paper tube. Fold the excess edges inside the paper tube and glue. Add rickrack if desired. Let dry.

5. Glue the pumpkins to the napkin rings. Let dry.

Carefully cut up the
toilet paper tube . . .

Make the pumpkins
for the front . . .

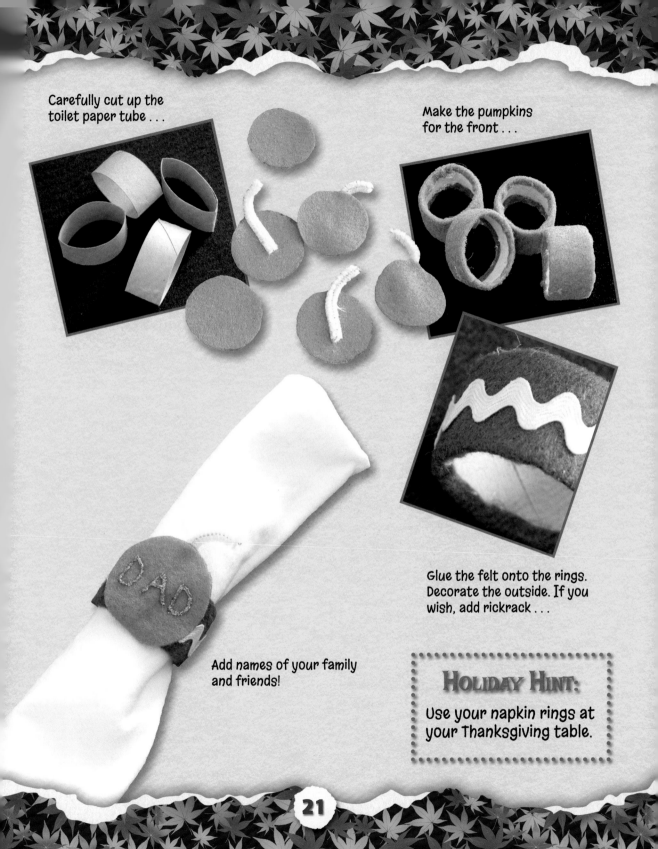

Glue the felt onto the rings.
Decorate the outside. If you
wish, add rickrack . . .

Add names of your family
and friends!

Thankfulness Book

Think about the people and things for which you are thankful. Write about them in this book. You can illustrate it, too.

What you will need

- scissors
- construction paper in orange and another color
- paper edger (optional)
- hole punch
- green pipe cleaners
- yarn or ribbon in a fall color
- white paper
- glue
- stickers, glitter, and/or bits of Thanksgiving confetti
- crayons
- pen or pencil

What to do

1. Cut two sheets of construction paper into 6- by 9-inch pieces. These will be the covers of your book. Cut a pumpkin shape from the orange paper. Add the pipe cleaner to make a stem for your pumpkin.

2. Decorate the cover with stickers, glitter, and Thanksgiving confetti. You can cut out your own designs and glue them on, too. Glue on yarn or ribbon to form a border.

3. Line up the sheets of paper that form the cover of your book. Punch holes so that they match. Punch the white paper to match the holes. You may need adult help for this. Poke the yarn or ribbon through the holes and tie.

4. Write about something that you are thankful for on each page. Draw pictures to illustrate your thoughts.

Glue a pumpkin to the front cover . . .

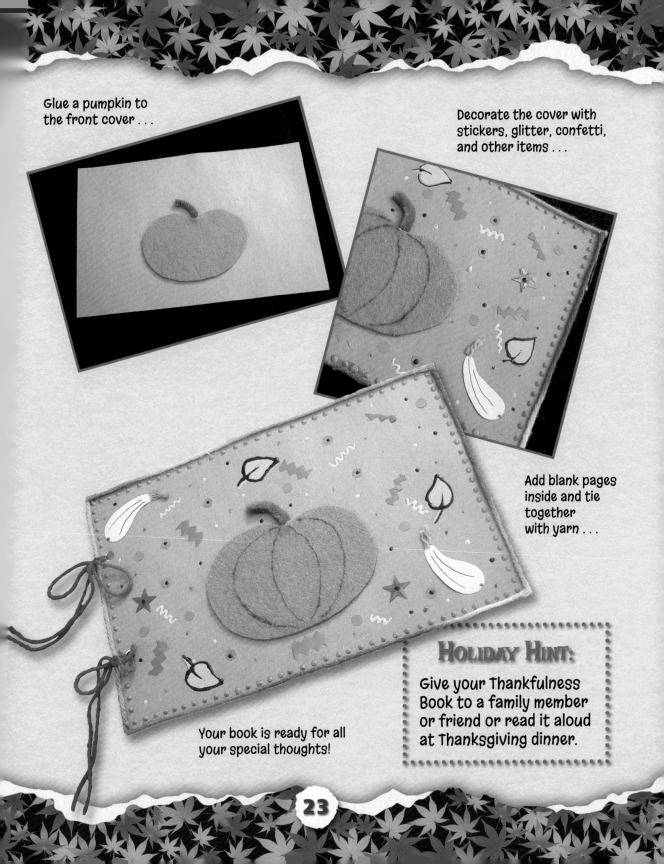

Decorate the cover with stickers, glitter, confetti, and other items . . .

Add blank pages inside and tie together with yarn . . .

Your book is ready for all your special thoughts!

HOLIDAY HINT:

Give your Thankfulness Book to a family member or friend or read it aloud at Thanksgiving dinner.

Turkey Place Cards

These turkeys will show Thanksgiving guests where to sit at your holiday table.

What you will need

- scissors
- cupcake liners
- fine-tipped marker
- craft spoons
- index cards
- glue
- brown construction paper
- wiggle eyes
- scraps of red and orange paper

What to do

1. Glue the cupcake liners so that they overlap, as shown.

2. Trace onto red and orange paper the turkey's wattle and beak. You can use the pattern on page 26. Cut them out. Glue them to the craft spoon. Add the wiggle eyes. Let dry.

3. Cut out a half-circle from the brown construction paper for the turkey's body. Glue to the bottom of the spoon.

4. Write a guest's name on the craft spoon.

5. Cut the index card in half and fold it to form a stand for the place card. Glue it to the back of the turkey. Let dry.

Glue together two cupcake liners . . .

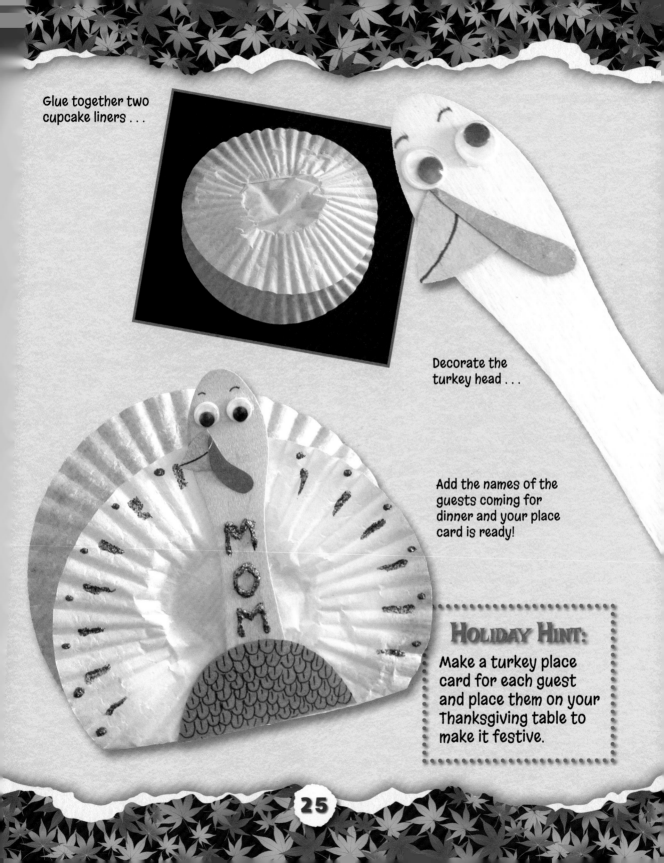

Decorate the turkey head . . .

Add the names of the guests coming for dinner and your place card is ready!

HOLIDAY HINT:

Make a turkey place card for each guest and place them on your Thanksgiving table to make it festive.

PATTERNS

Use tracing paper to copy the patterns on these pages. Ask an adult to help you cut and trace the shapes onto construction paper.

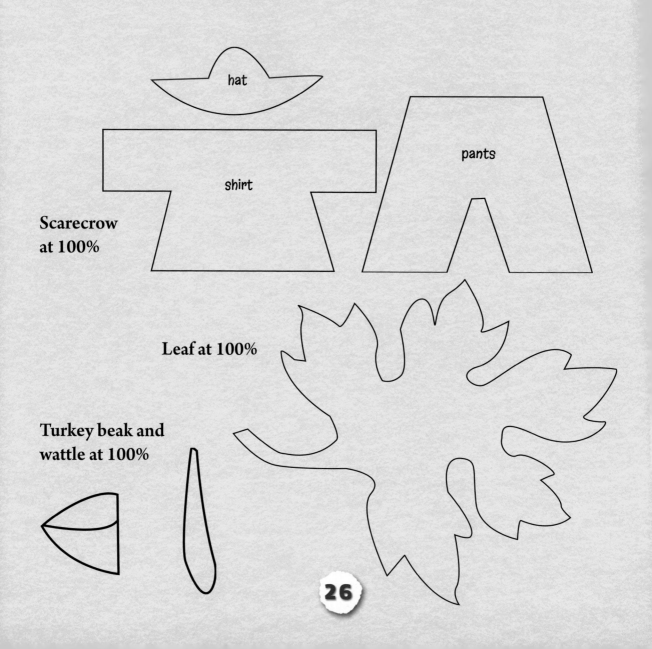

hat

shirt

pants

Scarecrow at 100%

Leaf at 100%

Turkey beak and wattle at 100%

Pilgrim clothes at 100%

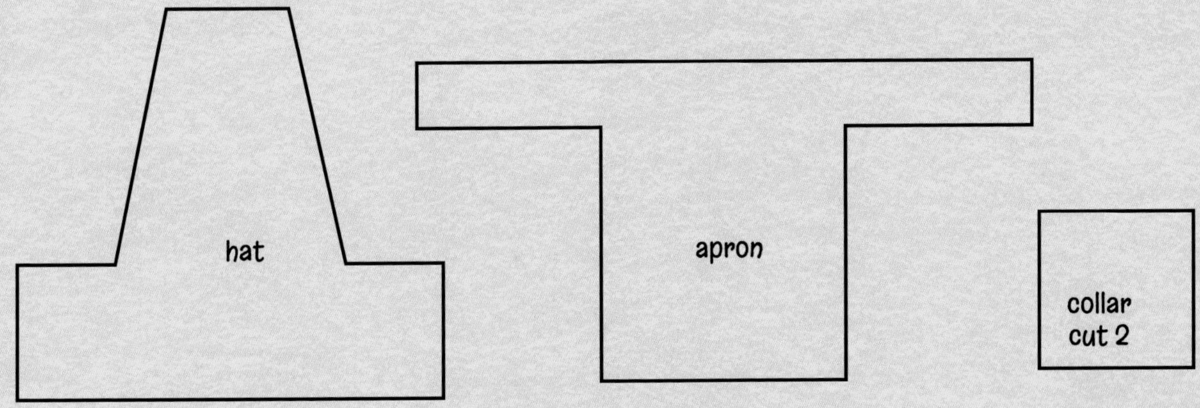

hat

apron

collar
cut 2

Mayfower sails at 100%

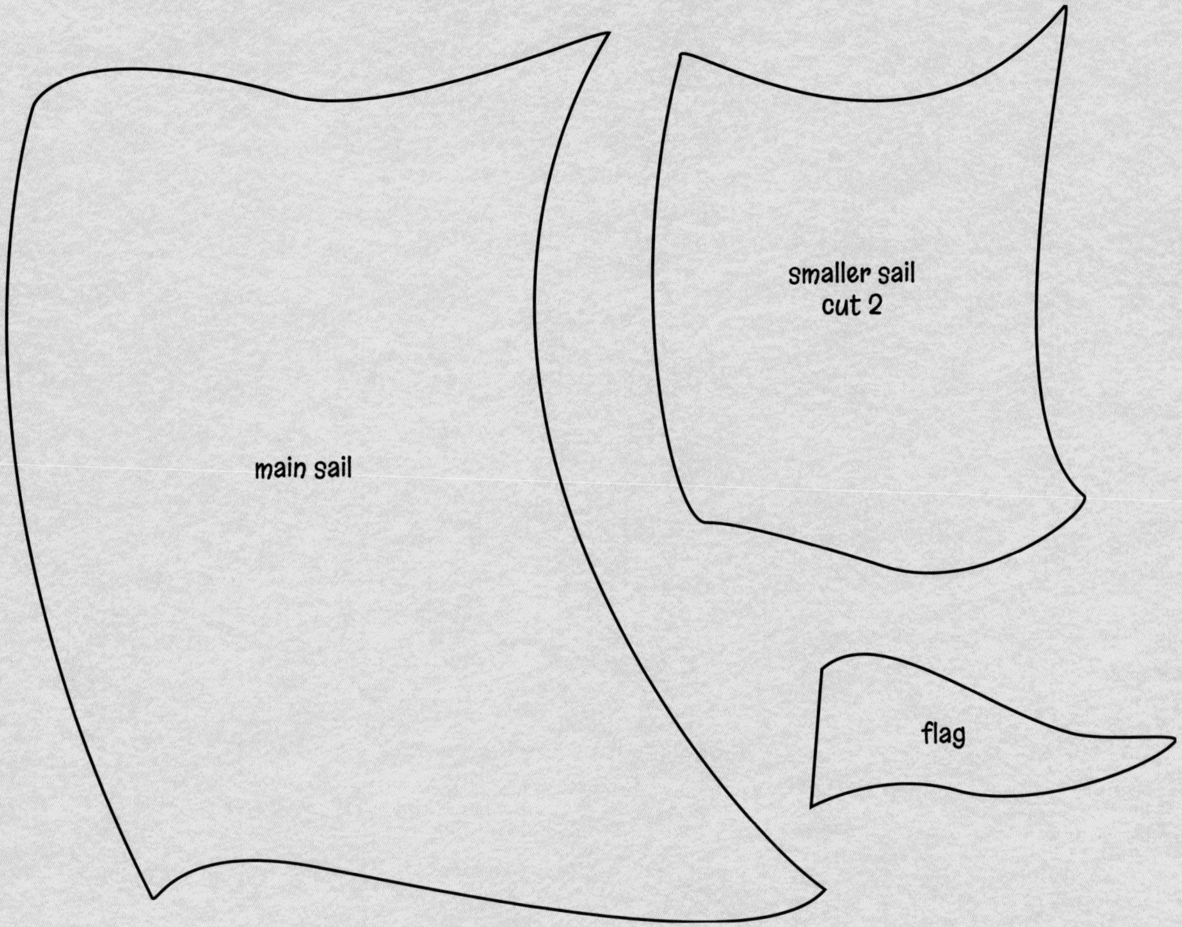

main sail

smaller sail
cut 2

flag

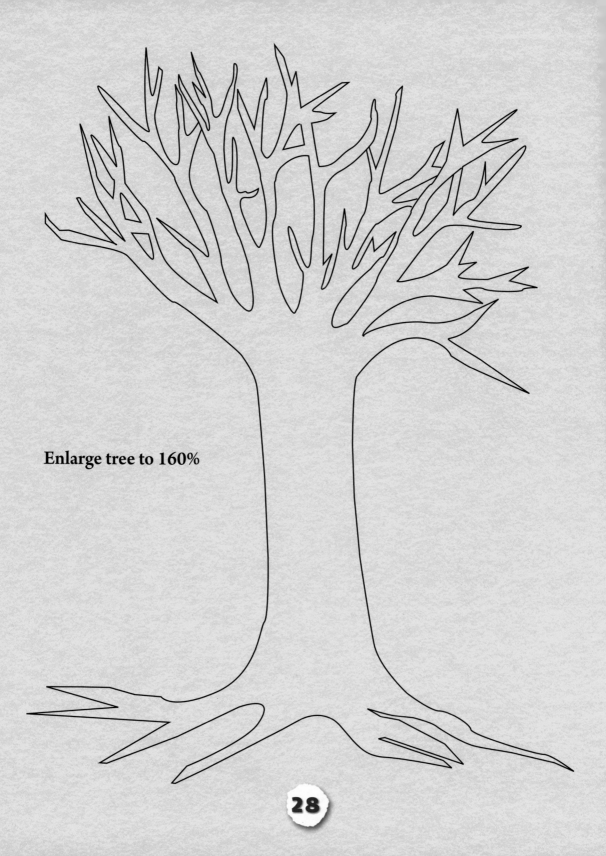

Enlarge tree to 160%

Words to Know

harvest—A gathering in of crops when they are ripe.

hull—The sides and bottom of a ship.

Mayflower—The ship that carried the first Pilgrims to America in 1620.

Pilgrims—The people who started a colony at Plymouth in New England in 1620.

scarecrow—A figure of a person used to frighten birds away from crops.

Thanksgiving—A holiday in the United States celebrated on the fourth Thursday in November to remember the first Pilgrims' harvest feast held in 1621.

tradition—The handing down of customs from parents to their children.

wattle—The skin that hangs from a turkey's neck.

READ ABOUT THANKSGIVING DAY

Anderson, Laurie Halse. *Thank You, Sara: The Woman Who Saved Thanksgiving*. New York: Simon & Schuster Books for Young Readers, 2002.

Arnosky, Jim. *All About Turkeys*. New York: Scholastic Press, 1998.

Landau, Elaine. *Thanksgiving: A Time to Be Thankful*. Berkeley Heights, N.J.: Enslow Publishers, Inc., 2001.

Roop, Connie, and Peter Roop. *Let's Celebrate Thanksgiving*. Brookfield, Conn.: Millbrook Press, 1999.

Rosinsky, Natalie M. *Thanksgiving*. Minneapolis, Minn.: Compass Point Books, 2003.

Schuh, Mari C. *Thanksgiving Day*. Mankato, Minn.: Pebble Books, 2003.

Swamp, Chief Jake. *Giving Thanks: A Native American Good Morning Message*. New York: Lee & Low Books, 1995.

INDEX